Thank you!
All good things & love,
Blessings
Pam

This journal belongs to

....

You are a beautiful woman of God,

precious to Him in every way. As you seek Him,
He will show you the mysteries of life and unfold
His unique plans for you—a life full of rich blessing.

God cares about you and knows all the desires of
your heart. He is as close as breathing.
Let this journal inspire you to express your
thoughts, record your prayers, embrace your
dreams, and listen to what God is saying to you.

Be strong in the Lord, and may His peace
guide your heart always.

Promises for Me
A PROMISE JOURNAL

...inspired by life

A Heart Full of Grace

Have you ever thought that in every action of grace in your heart you have the whole omnipotence of God engaged to bless you?

ANDREW MURRAY

> *I praise the Lord because he advises me.*
> *Even at night, I feel his leading.*
> *I keep the Lord before me always.*
> *Because he is close by my side,*
> *I will not be hurt.*
> *So I rejoice and am glad.*
> *Even my body has hope,*
> *because you will not leave me.*

PSALM 16:7-10 NCV

Look deep within yourself and recognize what brings life and grace into your heart. It is this that can be shared with those around you. You are loved by God. This is an inspiration to love.

CHRISTOPHER DE VINCK

There is no rest in the heart of God until
He knows that we are at rest in His grace.

LLOYD JOHN OGILVIE

....

....

....

....

....

....

....

....

....

....

....

....

Special Plans

This is the real gift: you have been given the breath of life, designed with a unique, one-of-a-kind soul that exists forever—the way that you choose to live it doesn't change the fact that you've been given the gift of being now and forever. Priceless in value, you are handcrafted by God, who has a personal design and plan for each of us.

WENDY MOORE

May God's love guide you through the special plans He has for your life.

Allow your dreams a place in your prayers and plans. God-given dreams can help you move into the future He is preparing for you.

Promises for Me

The LORD will work out his plans for my life—
for your faithful love, O LORD, endures forever.

PSALM 138:8 NLT

Wonderful Love

Show the wonder of your great love.... Keep me as the apple of your eye; hide me in the shadow of your wings.

PSALM 17:7-8 NIV

Give thanks to the LORD, for he is good! His faithful love endures forever.

PSALM 136:1 NLT

The Lord is kind and shows mercy.
He does not become angry quickly but is full of love.
The Lord is good to everyone;
he is merciful to all he has made.
Lord, everything you have made will praise you;
those who belong to you will bless you.
They will tell about the glory of your kingdom
and will speak about your power.
Then everyone will know the mighty things you do.

PSALM 145:8-12 NCV

Promises for Me

Every one of us as human beings is known and loved by the Creator apart from every other human on earth.

JAMES DOBSON

....
....
....
....
....
....
....
....
....
....
....
....

Encouragement Is Awesome

Oh, the comfort, the inexpressible comfort of feeling safe with a person—having neither to weigh thoughts nor measure words, but pouring them all right out just as they are, chaff and grain together, certain that a faithful hand will take and sift them, keep what is worth keeping and then, with the breath of kindness, blow the rest away.

DINAH MARIA MULOCK CRAIK

My purpose is that they may be encouraged in heart and united in love, so that they may have the full riches of complete understanding, in order that they may know the mystery of God.

COLOSSIANS 2:2-3 NIV

Some days, it is enough encouragement just to watch the clouds break up and disappear, leaving behind a blue patch of sky and bright sunshine that is so warm upon my face. It's a glimpse of divinity; a kiss from heaven.

WENDY MOORE

Encouragement is awesome.
It has the capacity to...actually change the
course of another human being's day, week, or life.

CHARLES R. SWINDOLL

Child of God

When we call on God, He bends down His ear to listen, as a father bends down to listen to his little child.

ELIZABETH CHARLES

He only is the Maker
of all things near and far;
He paints the wayside flower,
He lights the evening star;
the wind and waves obey Him,
by Him the birds are fed;
much more to us, His children,
He gives our daily bread.

MATTHIAS CLAUDIUS

Remember you are very special to God as His precious child. He has promised to complete the good work He has begun in you. As you continue to grow in Him, He will make you a blessing to others.

GARY SMALLEY AND JOHN TRENT

How great is the love the Father has lavished on us, that we should be called children of God! And that is what we are!

1 JOHN 3:1 NIV

Special Gifts

Every person ever created is so special that their presence in the world makes it richer and fuller and more wonderful than it could ever have been without them.

We were not sent into this world to do anything into which we cannot put our hearts.

JOHN RUSKIN

Use what talents you possess: the woods would be very silent if no birds sang there except those that sang best.

HENRY VAN DYKE

God gives everyone a special gift and a special place to use it.

*Where you are right now is God's place for you.
Live and obey and love and believe right there.*

1 CORINTHIANS 7:17 THE MESSAGE

Joy Personified

For the Kingdom of God is not a matter of what we eat or drink, but of living a life of goodness and peace and joy in the Holy Spirit. If you serve Christ with this attitude, you will please God, and others will approve of you, too. So then, let us aim for harmony in the church and try to build each other up.

ROMANS 14:17-19 NLT

The sun does not shine for a few trees and flowers, but for the wide world's joy.

HENRY WARD BEECHER

Promises for Me

As we grow in our capacities to see and enjoy the joys that God has placed in our lives, life becomes a glorious experience of discovering His endless wonders.

God's Heart

The LORD your God is with you....
He will take great delight in you,
he will quiet you with his love,
he will rejoice over you with singing.

ZEPHANIAH 3:17 NIV

There is no need to plead that the love of God shall fill our
hearts as though He were unwilling to fill us.... Love is
pressing around us on all sides like air. Cease to resist it
and instantly love takes possession.

AMY CARMICHAEL

God's heart is the most sensitive and tender of all. No act goes unnoticed, no matter how insignificant or small.

RICHARD J. FOSTER

Embraced by His Love

To be grateful is to recognize the love of God in everything He has given us—and He has given us everything. Every breath we draw is a gift of His love, every moment of existence a gift of grace.

THOMAS MERTON

You're blessed when you're at the end of your rope. With less of you there is more of God and his rule. You're blessed when you feel you've lost what is most dear to you. Only then can you be embraced by the One most dear to you.

MATTHEW 5:3-4 THE MESSAGE

Promises for Me

*God in His ample love embraces our love with...a sort of tenderness,
and we must tread the Way to Him hand in hand.*

SHELDON VANAUKEN

God Will Be My Guide

We do not understand the intricate pattern of the stars in their courses, but we know that He who created them does, and that just as surely as He guides them, He is charting a safe course for us.

Billy Graham

To be glad of life, because it gives you the chance to love and to work and to play and to look up at the stars; to be satisfied with your possessions, but not contented with yourself until you have made the best of them;...to think seldom of your enemies, often of your friends, and every day of Christ; and to spend as much time as you can, with body and with spirit in God's out-of-doors—these are little guideposts on the footpath to peace.

Henry van Dyke

*God shall be my hope, my stay,
my guide and lantern to my feet.*

William Shakespeare

But I'll take the hand of those who don't know the way, who can't see where they're going. I'll be a personal guide to them, directing them through unknown country.

ISAIAH 42:16 THE MESSAGE

The Gift of Miracles

Only He who created the wonders of the world entwines hearts in an eternal way.

Because of his great love for us, God, who is rich in mercy, made us alive with Christ even when we were dead in transgressions.... And God raised us up with Christ and seated us with him in the heavenly realms in Christ Jesus, in order that in the coming ages he might show the incomparable riches of his grace, expressed in his kindness to us in Christ Jesus.

EPHESIANS 2:4-7 NIV

There are only two ways to live your life.
One is as though nothing is a miracle.
The other is as though everything is a miracle.

RICHARD CRASHAW

I think miracles exist in part as gifts and in part as clues that there is something beyond the flat world we see.

PEGGY NOONAN

A Work of Art

Each one of us is God's special work of art. Through us, He teaches and inspires, delights and encourages, informs and uplifts all those who view our lives. God, the master artist, is most concerned about expressing Himself—His thoughts and His intentions—through what He paints in our character.... [He] wants to paint a beautiful portrait of His Son in and through your life. A painting like no other in all of time.

JONI EARECKSON TADA

Whether we are poets or parents or teachers or artists or gardeners, we must start where we are and use what we have. In the process of creation and relationship, what seems mundane and trivial may show itself to be holy, precious, part of a pattern.

LUCI SHAW

*I will give thanks to You, for I am fearfully and
wonderfully made; wonderful are Your works.*

PSALM 139:14 NASB

God's Workmanship

Every time Jesus sees that there is a possibility of giving us more than we know how to ask for, He does so.

OLE HALLESBY

For it is by grace you have been saved, through faith— and this not from yourselves, it is the gift of God—not by works, so that no one can boast. For we are God's workmanship, created in Christ Jesus to do good works, which God prepared in advance for us to do.

EPHESIANS 2:8-10 NIV

*As God's workmanship, we deserve to be treated, and to treat
ourselves, with affection and affirmation, regardless of our
appearance or performance.*

MARY ANN MAYO

....

....

....

....

....

....

....

....

....

....

....

Enfolded in Peace

I will let God's peace infuse every part of today. As the chaos swirls and life's demands pull at me on all sides, I will breathe in God's peace that surpasses all understanding. He has promised that He would set within me a peace too deeply planted to be affected by unexpected or exhausting demands.

Calm me, O Lord, as You stilled the storm,
Still me, O Lord, keep me from harm.
Let all the tumult within me cease,
Enfold me, Lord, in Your peace.

CELTIC TRADITIONAL

God cannot give us a happiness and peace apart from Himself, because it is not there. There is no such thing.
C. S. LEWIS

Don't worry about anything; instead, pray about everything.
Tell God what you need, and thank him for all he has done.
Then you will experience God's peace, which exceeds anything
we can understand. His peace will guard your hearts
and minds as you live in Christ Jesus.

PHILIPPIANS 4:6-7 NLT

Unconditional Love

There is nothing we can do that will make God love us less, and there's nothing we can do that will make Him love us more. He will always and forever love us unconditionally. What He wants from us is that we love Him back with all our heart.

Do not dwell upon your inner failings.... Just do this: Bring your soul to the Great Physician—exactly as you are, even and especially at your worst moment.... For it is in such moments that you will most readily sense His healing presence.

TERESA OF AVILA

*My grace is sufficient for you, for My strength
is made perfect in weakness.*

2 CORINTHIANS 12:9 NKJV

God Cares About Your Everythings

We are never more fulfilled than when our longing for God is met by His presence in our lives.

BILLY GRAHAM

The love of the Father is like a sudden rain shower that will pour forth when you least expect it, catching you up into wonder and praise.

RICHARD J. FOSTER

Your Father knows the things you need before you ask him. So when you pray, you should pray like this: "Our Father in heaven, may your name always be kept holy. May your kingdom come and what you want be done, here on earth as it is in heaven."

MATTHEW 6:8-10 NCV

Tuck [this] thought into your heart today. Treasure it. Your Father God cares about your daily everythings that concern you.

KAY ARTHUR

Every Day Is a Gift to Cherish

Everything in life is most fundamentally a gift. And you receive it best, and you live it best, by holding it with very open hands.

LEO O'DONOVAN

Go after a life of love as if your life depended on it— because it does. Give yourselves to the gifts God gives you. Most of all, try to proclaim his truth.

1 CORINTHIANS 14:1 THE MESSAGE

Every day we live is a priceless gift of God, loaded with possibilities to learn something new, to gain fresh insights.

DALE EVANS ROGERS

Time is a very precious gift of God; so precious
that it's only given to us moment by moment.

AMELIA BARR

A Fountain of Gladness

The wise are known for their understanding. Their pleasant words make them better teachers. Understanding is like a fountain which gives life to those who use it.

Proverbs 16:21-22 NCV

Kindness has been described in many ways. It is the poetry of the heart, the music of the world. It is the golden chain which binds society together. It is a fountain of gladness.

The War Cry

Happy is the person who trusts the Lord....
Lord my God, you have done many miracles.
Your plans for us are many.
If I tried to tell them all,
there would be too many to count.

Psalm 40:4-6 NCV

*A kind heart is a fountain of gladness, making
everything in its vicinity freshen into smiles.*
WASHINGTON IRVING

Restoration

The Spirit of the Sovereign LORD is upon me,
for the LORD has anointed me
to bring good news to the poor.
He has sent me to comfort the brokenhearted
and to proclaim that captives will be released
and prisoners will be freed.
He has sent me to tell those who mourn
that the time of the LORD's favor has come,
and with it, the day of God's anger against their enemies.
To all who mourn in Israel,
he will give a crown of beauty for ashes,
a joyous blessing instead of mourning,
festive praise instead of despair.
In their righteousness, they will be like great oaks
that the LORD has planted for his own glory.

ISAIAH 61:1-3 NLT

*The Lord promises to bind up the brokenhearted,
to give relief and full deliverance to those whose spirits
have been weighed down.*

CHARLES R. SWINDOLL

Created to Love

Love loves to be told what it knows already.... It wants to be asked for what it longs to give.

PETER TAYLOR FORSYTH

Love must be sincere. Hate what is evil; cling to what is good. Be devoted to one another in brotherly love. Honor one another above yourselves.

ROMANS 12:9-10 NIV

Who we are is connected to those we love and to those who have influenced us toward goodness.

CHRISTOPHER DE VINCK

*Caring words, friendship, affectionate touch—
all of these have a healing quality. Why? Because we
were all created by God to give and receive love.*

JACK FROST

Blessings Await

Having someone who understands is a great blessing for ourselves. Being someone who understands is a great blessing to others.

JANETTE OKE

Lift up your eyes. Your heavenly Father waits to bless you—in inconceivable ways to make your life what you never dreamed it could be.

ANNE ORTLUND

And God can give you more blessings than you need. Then you will always have plenty of everything— enough to give to every good work.

2 CORINTHIANS 9:8 NCV

Some blessings—like rainbows after rain or a friend's listening ear—are extraordinary gifts waiting to be discovered in an ordinary day.

A Countenance Made Beautiful

Joy is the echo of God's life within us.
JOSEPH MARMION

God has made everything beautiful for its own time. He has planted eternity in the human heart.
ECCLESIASTES 3:11 NLT

Into all our lives, in simple, familiar, homely ways, God infuses this element of joy from the surprises of life, which unexpectedly brighten our days and fill our eyes with light.
HENRY WADSWORTH LONGFELLOW

Think of all the beauty still left around you and be happy.
ANNE FRANK

As a countenance is made beautiful by the soul's shining through it, so the world is beautiful by the shining through it of God.

FRIEDRICH HEINRICH JACOBI

A Splendid Gift

This bright, new day, complete with twenty-four hours of opportunities, choices, and attitudes comes with a perfectly matched set of 1,440 minutes. This unique gift, this one day, cannot be exchanged, replaced, or refunded. Handle with care. Make the most of it. There is only one to a customer!

You have a unique message to deliver, a unique song to sing, a unique act of love to bestow. This message, this song, and this act of love have been entrusted exclusively to the one and only you.

JOHN POWELL, S.J.

Isn't everything you have *and everything you* are *sheer gifts from God?*

1 CORINTHIANS 4:7 THE MESSAGE

*Live your life while you have it. Life is a splendid gift—
there is nothing small about it.*

FLORENCE NIGHTINGALE

....

....

....

....

....

....

....

....

....

....

....

Dear God...

You are a child of your heavenly Father. Confide in Him.
Your faith in His love and power can never be bold enough.

BASILEA SCHLINK

Where are you? Start there. Openly and freely declare your
need to the One who cares deeply.

CHARLES R. SWINDOLL

We must take our troubles to the Lord, but we must do
more than that; we must leave them there.

HANNAH WHITALL SMITH

Embrace this God-life. Really embrace it, and nothing will
be too much for you.... That's why I urge you to pray for
absolutely everything, ranging from small to large. Include
everything as you embrace this God-life, and you'll get
God's everything.

MARK 11:22-24 THE MESSAGE

You pay God a compliment by asking great things of Him.
TERESA OF AVILA

....

....

....

....

....

....

....

....

....

....

....

The Most Important Times

You will find as you look back upon your life, that the moments when you have really lived are the moments when you have done things in the spirit of love.

HENRY DRUMMOND

He redeems me from death
and crowns me with love and tender mercies.
He fills my life with good things.
My youth is renewed like the eagle's!

PSALM 103:4-5 NLT

Stand outside this evening. Look at the stars. Know that you are special and loved by the One who created them.

*Moments spent listening, talking, playing, and sharing together
may be the most important times of all.*

GLORIA GAITHER

Designed on Purpose

It's in Christ that we find out who we are and what we are living for. Long before we first heard of Christ and got our hopes up, he had his eye on us, had designs on us for glorious living, part of the overall purpose he is working out in everything and everyone.

EPHESIANS 1:11-12 THE MESSAGE

To every thing there is a season,
A time for every purpose under the heaven.

ECCLESIASTES 3:1 NKJV

All the days ordained for me were written in your book before one of them came to be.

PSALM 139:15-16 NIV

I delight to do Your will, O my God.

PSALM 40:8 NKJV

*The patterns of our days are always rearranging...
and each design for living is unique, graced with its
own special beauty.*

The Love of God

Can anything ever separate us from Christ's love? Does it mean he no longer loves us if we have trouble or calamity, or are persecuted, or hungry, or destitute, or in danger, or threatened with death?... No, despite all these things, overwhelming victory is ours through Christ, who loved us. And I am convinced that nothing can ever separate us from God's love. Neither death nor life, neither angels nor demons, neither our fears for today nor our worries about tomorrow—not even the powers of hell can separate us from God's love.

Romans 8:35-36, 38 NLT

Promises for Me

*Nothing can separate you from His love, absolutely nothing....
God is enough for time, and God is enough
for eternity. God is enough!*

HANNAH WHITALL SMITH

Simple and Natural Things

The splendor of the rose and the whiteness of the lily do not rob the little violet of its scent nor the daisy of its simple charm. If every tiny flower wanted to be a rose, spring would lose its loveliness.

THÉRÈSE OF LISIEUX

I pray that you may enjoy good health and that all may go well with you, even as your soul is getting along well.

3 JOHN 1:2 NIV

Happy people...enjoy the fundamental, often very simple things of life.... They savor the moment, glad to be alive, enjoying their work, their families, the good things around them.... Their eyes are turned outward; they are aware, compassionate. They have the capacity to love.

JANE CANFIELD

From the simple seeds of understanding,
we reap the lovely harvest of true friendship.

....

....

....

....

....

....

....

....

....

....

....

....

Treasure Today

See each morning a world made anew, as if it were the morning of the very first day;...treasure and use it, as if it were the final hour of the very last day.

FAY HARTZELL ARNOLD

For the LORD grants wisdom!
From his mouth come knowledge and understanding.
He grants a treasure of common sense to the honest.
He is a shield to those who walk with integrity.
He guards the paths of the just
and protects those who are faithful to him.
Then you will understand what is right, just, and fair,
and you will find the right way to go.

PROVERBS 2:6-9 NLT

In ordinary life we hardly realize that we receive a great deal more than we give, and that it is only with gratitude that life becomes rich.

DIETRICH BONHOEFFER

Normal day, let me be aware of the treasure you are. Let me learn from you, love you, bless you before you depart. Let me not pass you by in quest of some rare and perfect tomorrow.

Love Wrapped up for You

But me he caught—reached all the way

from sky to sea; he pulled me out

Of that ocean of hate, that enemy chaos,

the void in which I was drowning.

They hit me when I was down,

but GOD stuck by me.

He stood me up on a wide-open field;

I stood there saved—surprised to be loved!

PSALM 18:18-19 THE MESSAGE

*

Each day is a treasure box of gifts from God, just waiting to be opened. Open your gifts with excitement. You will find forgiveness attached to ribbons of joy. You will find love wrapped in sparkling gems.

JOAN CLAYTON

....

....

....

....

....

....

....

....

....

....

....

God Hears

We can now come fearlessly into God's presence,
assured of his glad welcome.

EPHESIANS 3:12 NLT

I love those who love Me;
And those who diligently seek Me will find Me.
Riches and honor are with Me,
Enduring wealth and righteousness.
My fruit is better than gold, even pure gold,
And my yield better than choicest silver.

PROVERBS 8:17-19 NASB

One single grateful thought raised to heaven is the most
perfect prayer.

G. E. LESSING

No matter where we are, God can hear us from there!

The Giving Heart

Give, and it will be given to you. A good measure, pressed down, shaken together and running over, will be poured into your lap. For with the measure you use, it will be measured to you.

LUKE 6:38 NIV

The heart hath its own memory,
like the mind,
And in it are enshrined
The precious keepsakes,
into which is wrought
The giver's loving thought.

HENRY WADSWORTH LONGFELLOW

✳

Promises for Me

*A smile is a light in the window of the soul
indicating that the heart is at home.*

Seek First

Why do you worry about clothes? Look at how the lilies in the field grow. They don't work or make clothes for themselves. But I tell you that even Solomon with his riches was not dressed as beautifully as one of these flowers. God clothes the grass in the field, which is alive today but tomorrow is thrown into the fire. So you can be even more sure that God will clothe you. Don't have so little faith! Don't worry and say, "What will we eat?" or "What will we drink?" or "What will we wear?" The people who don't know God keep trying to get these things, and your Father in heaven knows you need them. Seek first God's kingdom and what God wants. Then all your other needs will be met as well.

MATTHEW 6:28-33 NCV

Trust the past to the mercy of God, the present to His love, and the future to His Providence.

AUGUSTINE

Love Conquers All

Love grows from our capacity to give what is deepest within ourselves and also receive what is the deepest within another person. The heart becomes an ocean strong and deep, launching all on its tide.

For great is his love toward us, and the faithfulness of the LORD endures forever.

PSALM 117:2 NIV

Love is that condition in which the happiness of another person is essential to your own.

ROBERT A. HEINLEIN

Before anything else, above all else, beyond everything else, God loves us. God loves us extravagantly, ridiculously, without limit or condition. God is in love with us...God yearns for us.

ROBERTA BONDI

*God has called us into the joyous ministry
of giving His love away to others.*
DON LESSIN

Fear Not

Don't be afraid, I've redeemed you.
I've called your name. You're mine.
When you're in over your head, I'll be there with you.
When you're in rough waters, you will not go down.
When you're between a rock and a hard place,
it won't be a dead end—
Because I am GOD, your personal God,
The Holy of Israel, your Savior.
I paid a huge price for you…!
That's how much you mean to me!
That's how much I love you!

ISAIAH 43:1-4 THE MESSAGE

If God is for us, who is against us? He who did not spare
His own Son, but delivered Him over for us all, how will
He not also with Him freely give us all things?

ROMANS 8:31-32 NASB

Do not be afraid to enter the cloud that is settling down on your life. God is in it. The other side is radiant with His glory.

L. B. COWMAN

A Life of Purpose

God not only knows us, but He values us highly in spite of all He knows.... You and I are the creatures He prizes above the rest of His creation. We are made in His image and He sacrificed His Son that each one of us might be one with Him.

JOHN FISHER

I believe that nothing that happens to me is meaningless, and that it is good for us all that it should be so, even if it runs counter to our own wishes. As I see it, I'm here for some purpose, and I only hope I may fulfill it.

DIETRICH BONHOEFFER

*And we know that all things work together for good
to those who love God, to those who are the called
according to His purpose.*

ROMANS 8:28 NKJV

In God's Design

God has designs on our future...and He has designed us for the future. He has given us something to do in the future that no one else can do.

RUTH SENTER

Your life is a journey you must travel with a deep consciousness of God. It cost God plenty to get you out of that dead-end, empty-headed life you grew up in. He paid with Christ's sacred blood, you know.... It's because of this sacrificed Messiah...that you trust God, that you know you have a future in God.

I PETER 1:18-21 THE MESSAGE

God wants to continually add to us, to develop and enlarge us—always building on what He has already taught and built in us.

A. B. SIMPSON

Never be afraid to trust an unknown future to a known God.
CORRIE TEN BOOM

....

....

....

....

....

....

....

....

....

....

....

A Faith Lifestyle

You're blessed when you get your inside world—your mind and heart—put right. Then you can see God in the outside world.

MATTHEW 5:8 THE MESSAGE

Nothing is so strong as gentleness, and nothing so gentle as real strength.

FRANCIS DE SALES

Pursue righteousness, godliness, faith, love, endurance and gentleness. Fight the good fight of the faith. Take hold of the eternal life to which you were called when you made your good confession in the presence of many witnesses.

1 TIMOTHY 6:11-12 NIV

The human contribution is the essential ingredient. It is only in the giving of oneself to others that we truly live.

ETHEL PERCY ANDRUS

Spirituality is not one compartment or sphere of life. Rather, it is a lifestyle: the process of life lived with the vision of faith.

BRENNAN MANNING

Share the Secret

Know that I'm on your side, right alongside you. You're not in this alone. I want you woven into a tapestry of love, in touch with everything there is to know of God. Then you will have minds confident and at rest, focused on Christ, God's great mystery. All the richest treasures of wisdom and knowledge are embedded in that mystery and nowhere else.

COLOSSIANS 2:1-2 THE MESSAGE

The real secret of happiness is not what you give or what you receive, it's what you share.

> *To be able to find joy in another's joy,*
> *that is the secret of happiness.*

*The secret of life is that all we have and
are is a gift of grace to be shared.*

LLOYD JOHN OGILVIE

Small Differences

It is not my business to think about myself. My business is to think about God. It is for God to think about me.

SIMONE WEIL

Whatever is true, whatever is noble, whatever is right, whatever is pure, whatever is lovely, whatever is admirable—if anything is excellent or praiseworthy— think about such things.

PHILIPPIANS 4:8 NIV

We must not, in trying to think about how we can make a big difference, ignore the small daily differences we can make which, over time, add up to big differences that we often cannot foresee.

MARIAN WRIGHT EDELMAN

Promises for Me

As a rose fills a room with its fragrance,
so will God's love fill our lives.
MARGARET BROWNLEY

....

....

....

....

....

....

....

....

....

....

Completely Loved

You are valuable just because you exist. Not because of what you do or what you have done, but simply because you are. Just think about the way Jesus honors you...and smile.
MAX LUCADO

What good news! God knows me completely and still loves me.

We are of such value to God that He came to live among us...and to guide us home. He will go to any length to seek us.... We can only respond by loving God for His love.
CATHERINE OF SIENA

We love Him because He first loved us.
1 JOHN 4:19 NKJV

Hidden Things

Solitude, silence, ordinary tasks,
being with people without great agendas,
sleeping, eating, working, playing...
all of that without being different from others,
that is the life that Jesus lived
and the life He asks us to live....

Even during His active ministry,
Jesus continued to return to hidden places
to be alone with God.

If we don't have a hidden life with God,
our public life for God cannot bear fruit.

HENRI J. M. NOUWEN

Praise be to the name of God for ever and ever....
He reveals deep and hidden things; he knows what
lies in darkness, and light dwells with him.

DANIEL 2:20–22 NIV

True silence is the rest of the mind; it is to the spirit what sleep is to the body, nourishment and refreshment.
WILLIAM PENN

God Knows You

God knows everything about us. And He cares about everything. Moreover, He can manage every situation. And He loves us! Surely this is enough to open the wellsprings of joy.... And joy is always a source of strength.

HANNAH WHITALL SMITH

*O Lord, you have examined my heart
and know everything about me.
You know when I sit down or stand up.
You know my thoughts even when I'm far away.
You see me when I travel
and when I rest at home.
You know everything I do.
You know what I am going to say....
You go before me and follow me.
You place your hand of blessing on my head.*

PSALM 139:1-5 NLT

God created the universe, but He also created you.
God knows you, God loves you, and God cares about the
tiniest details of your life.

BRUCE BICKEL AND STAN JANTZ

Contentment

I have learned to be content in whatever circumstances I am. I know how to get along with humble means, and I also know how to live in prosperity; in any and every circumstance I have learned the secret of being filled and going hungry, both of having abundance and suffering need. I can do all things through Him who strengthens me.

PHILIPPIANS 4:11-13 NASB

Be content with who you are, and don't put on airs. God's strong hand is on you; he'll promote you at the right time. Live carefree before God; he is most careful with you.

1 PETER 5:6-7 THE MESSAGE

Godliness with contentment is great gain. For we brought nothing into the world, and we can take nothing out of it. But if we have food and clothing, we will be content with that.

1 TIMOTHY 6:6-8 NIV

Contentment is not the fulfillment of what you want,
but the realization of how much you already have.

His Beautiful World

The God who holds the whole world in His hands wraps Himself in the splendor of the sun's light and walks among the clouds.

*Forbid that I should walk through Thy beautiful world
    with unseeing eyes:*
*Forbid that the lure of the market-place should ever
    entirely steal my heart away from the love of the
    open acres and the green trees:*
*Forbid that under the low roof of workshop or office or
    study I should ever forget Thy great overarching sky.*

JOHN BAILLIE

The whole earth is full of His glory!

ISAIAH 6:3 NKJV

Our Creator would never have made such lovely days, and given us the deep hearts to enjoy them, above and beyond all thought, unless we were meant to be immortal.

NATHANIEL HAWTHORNE

Valuable Treasure

Friendship is unnecessary, like philosophy, like art.... It has no survival value; rather it is one of those things that give value to survival.

C. S. Lewis

Only where the heart is can the treasure be found.

Sir James M. Barrie

For where your treasure is, there will your heart be also.

Matthew 6:21 niv

Out of your relationship with God come life's greatest treasures—fellowship, wisdom, peacefulness of soul, eternal hope, gladness of heart, direction and meaning, and a glorious purpose in all you do.

Roy Lessin

Memories, important yesterdays, were once todays.
Treasure and notice today.

GLORIA GAITHER

Totally Aware

*God is every moment totally aware of each one of us.
Totally aware in intense concentration and love.... No one
passes through any area of life, happy or tragic, without the
attention of God.*

EUGENIA PRICE

*If you have a special need today, focus your full attention
on the goodness and greatness of your Father rather than
on the size of your need. Your need is so small compared to
His ability to meet it.*

*May you have the power to understand, as all
God's people should, how wide, how long, how high,
and how deep his love is.*

EPHESIANS 3:18 NLT

Give It Away

You're here to be light, bringing out the God-colors in the world. God is not a secret to be kept. We're going public with this, as public as a city on a hill. If I make you light-bearers, you don't think I'm going to hide you under a bucket, do you? I'm putting you on a light stand. Now that I've put you there on a hilltop, on a light stand—shine! Keep open house; be generous with your lives. By opening up to others, you'll prompt people to open up with God, this generous Father in heaven.

MATTHEW 5:14 THE MESSAGE

The true meaning of life is to plant trees, under whose shade you do not expect to sit.

NELSON HENDERSON

Love in the heart wasn't put there to stay;
Love isn't love 'til you give it away.
OSCAR HAMMERSTEIN II

Made for Joy

Our hearts were made for joy. Our hearts were made to enjoy the One who created them. Too deeply planted to be much affected by the ups and downs of life, this joy is a knowing and a being known by our Creator. He sets our hearts alight with radiant joy.

WENDY MOORE

If one is joyful, it means that one is faithfully living for God, and that nothing else counts; and if one gives joy to others one is doing God's work. With joy without and joy within, all is well.

JANET ERSKINE STUART

Live for today but hold your hands open to tomorrow. Anticipate the future and its changes with joy. There is a seed of God's love in every event, every circumstance, every unpleasant situation in which you may find yourself.

BARBARA JOHNSON

The joy of the LORD is your strength.
NEHEMIAH 8:10 NKJV

New Possibilities

You see things as they are and ask, "Why?" I dream things as they never were and ask, "Why not?"

GEORGE BERNARD SHAW

We are made to reach out beyond our grasp.

OSWALD CHAMBERS

Happy are those who hear the joyful call to worship,
for they will walk in the light of your presence, Lord.
They rejoice all day long in your wonderful reputation.
They exult in your righteousness.
You are their glorious strength.
It pleases you to make us strong.

PSALM 89:15-17 NLT

Remember that happiness is a way of travel—
not a destination.

ROY M. GOODMAN

> *Most new discoveries are suddenly-seen*
> *things that were always there.*
> SUSANNE K. LANGER

Always There

God is always present in the temple of your heart...His home. And when you come in to meet Him there, you find that it is the one place of deep satisfaction where every longing is met.

Always be in a state of expectancy, and see that you leave room for God to come in as He likes.

OSWALD CHAMBERS

How lovely are Your dwelling places, O LORD of hosts! My soul longed and even yearned for the courts of the LORD; my heart and my flesh sing for joy to the living God....
For a day in Your courts is better than a thousand outside.

PSALM 84:1-2, 10 NASB

We need never shout across the spaces to an absent God. He is nearer than our own soul, closer than our most secret thoughts.

A. W. TOZER

Sanctuary of the Soul

Isn't it a wonderful morning? The world looks like something God had just imagined for His own pleasure.

LUCY MAUD MONTGOMERY

The meaning of earthly existence lies, not as we have grown used to thinking, in prospering, but in the development of the soul.

ALEKSANDR SOLZHENITSYN

May the Lord direct your hearts into the love of God and into the steadfastness of Christ.

2 THESSALONIANS 3:4-5 NASB

God waits for us in the inner sanctuary of the soul.
He welcomes us there.

RICHARD J. FOSTER

Life is a Special Occasion

I would rather be ashes than dust! I would rather that my spark would burn out in a brilliant blaze than it should be stifled by dry rot. I would rather be a superb meteor, every atom of me in magnificent glow, than a sleepy and permanent planet. The proper function of man is to live, not to exist. I shall not waste my days in trying to prolong them. I shall use my time.

JACK LONDON

I can't tell you how much I long for you to enter this wide-open, spacious life.... Your lives aren't small, but you're living them in a small way. I'm speaking as plainly as I can and with great affection. Open up your lives. Live openly and expansively!

2 CORINTHIANS 6:11-13 THE MESSAGE

Bottom line, wasn't life itself a special occasion?
JAN KARON

You Are Incomparable

Since this is the kind of life we have chosen, the life of the Spirit, let us make sure that we do not just hold it as an idea in our heads or a sentiment in our hearts, but work out its implications in every detail of our lives. That means we will not compare ourselves with each other as if one of us were better and another worse. We have far more interesting things to do with our lives. Each of us is an original.

GALATIANS 5:25-26 THE MESSAGE

I know not where His islands lift
their fronded palms in air;
I only know I cannot drift
beyond His love and care.

JOHN GREENLEAF WHITTIER

Since you are like no other being ever created since the beginning of time, you are incomparable.
BRENDA UELAND

....

....

....

....

....

....

....

....

....

....

....

Faith

Now faith is being sure of what we hope for
and certain of what we do not see....
By faith we understand that
the universe was formed at God's command,
so that what is seen
was not made out of what was visible....
And without faith
it is impossible to please God,
because anyone who comes to him
must believe that he exists
and that he rewards those
who earnestly seek him.

HEBREWS 11:1, 3, 6 NIV

*

Great faith isn't the ability to believe long and far into the misty future. It's simply taking God at His word and taking the next step.

JONI EARECKSON TADA

A Love Letter from God

*God is so big He can cover the whole world with His love,
and so small He can curl up inside your heart.*

JUNE MASTERS BACHER

*He made the entire human race and made the earth
hospitable, with plenty of time and space for living so we
could seek after God, and not just grope around in the dark
but actually find him.... He's not remote; he's near.*

ACTS 17:26-27 THE MESSAGE

*Are you aware that the Father takes delight in you and
that He thinks about you all the time?*

JACK FROST

*All the things in this world are gifts
and signs of God's love to us. The whole world
is a love letter from God.*

PETER KREEFT

....

....

....

....

....

....

....

....

....

....

....

....

....

Free to Live

GOD, your God, will cut away the thick calluses on your heart and your children's hearts, freeing you to love GOD, your God, with your whole heart and soul and live, really live.... And you will make a new start, listening obediently to GOD, keeping all his commandments that I'm commanding you today. GOD, your God, will outdo himself in making things go well for you.... Love GOD, your God. Walk in his ways. Keep his commandments, regulations, and rules so that you will live, really live, live exuberantly, blessed by GOD.... Love GOD, your God, listening obediently to him, firmly embracing him. Oh yes, he is life itself.

DEUTERONOMY 30:6-9, 16, 20 THE MESSAGE

Promises for Me

I asked God for all things that I might enjoy life. He gave me life that I might enjoy all things.

God's Own Gift

I have learned that to have a good friend is the purest of all God's gifts, for it is a love that has no exchange of payment.
FRANCES FARMER

Blessed are they who have the gift of making friends, for it is one of God's best gifts.
THOMAS HUGHES

The fruit of the Spirit is love, joy, peace, patience, kindness, goodness, faithfulness, gentleness and self-control.
GALATIANS 5:22-23 NIV

Your friends are God's gift to you, just as you are His gift to them.

A true friend is the gift of God, and...He only who made hearts can unite them.
ROBERT SOUTH

*The friend given to you by circumstances over which
you have no control was God's own gift.*

FREDERICK ROBERTSON

....

....

....

....

....

....

....

....

....

....

....

....

....

Someone Special

The Creator thinks enough of you to have sent Someone very special so that you might have life—abundantly, joyfully, completely, and victoriously.

When we love someone, we want to be with them, and we view their love for us with great honor even if they are not a person of great status. For this reason—and not because of our great status—God values our love. So much, in fact, that He suffered greatly on our behalf.

JOHN CHRYSOSTOM

One of Jesus' specialties is to make somebodies out of nobodies.

HENRIETTA MEARS

*God demonstrates His own love toward us, in that
while we were yet sinners, Christ died for us.*

ROMANS 5:8 NASB

An Instrument of Peace

Lord, make me an instrument of Thy peace.
Where there is hatred, let me sow love;
Where there is injury, pardon;
Where there is doubt, faith;
Where there is despair, hope;
Where there is darkness, light;
Where there is sadness, joy....

Grant that I may not so much seek
to be consoled as to console,
to be understood as to understand,
to be loved as to love.

For it is in giving that we receive,
It is in pardoning that we are pardoned,
And it is in dying that we are born to eternal life.

FRANCIS OF ASSISI

Peace I leave with you, My peace I give unto you....
Let not your heart be troubled, neither let it be afraid.

JOHN 14:27 NKJV

Near His Heart

*May God give you eyes to see beauty only the heart
can understand.*

*God loves you in the morning sun and the evening rain,
without caution or regret.*

BRENNAN MANNING

*Lord, your love reaches to the heavens, your loyalty
to the skies. Your goodness is as high as the mountains.
Your justice is as deep as the great ocean.*

PSALM 36:5-6 NCV

*God will never let you be shaken or moved from your place
near His heart.*

JONI EARECKSON TADA

Promises for Me

*The treasure our heart searches for is
found in the ocean of God's love.*
JANET WEAVER SMITH

Settled in Solitude

Solitude liberates us from entanglements by carving out a space from which we can see ourselves and our situation before the Audience of One. Solitude provides the private place where we can take our bearings and so make God our North Star.

Os Guinness

We must drink deeply from the very Source, the deep calm and peace of interior quietude and refreshment of God, allowing the pure water of divine grace to flow plentifully and unceasingly from the Source itself.

Mother Teresa

Whoever drinks of the water that I will give him shall never thirst; but the water that I will give him will become in him a well of water springing up to eternal life.

JOHN 4:13-14 NASB

Paths of Life

But the path of the righteous is like the light of dawn, that shines brighter and brighter until the full day.

PROVERBS 4:18 NASB

You have made known to me the paths of life; you will fill me with joy in your presence.

ACTS 2:28 NIV

Your word is a lamp to my feet
And a light to my path.

PSALM 119:105 NKJV

Come, let us go up to the mountain of the Lord.... There he will teach us his ways, and we will walk in his paths.

MICAH 4:2 NLT

*The best things are nearest...light in your eyes, flowers at your feet,
duties at your hand, the path of God just before you.*

ROBERT LOUIS STEVENSON

Dreams Fulfilled

God created us with an overwhelming desire to soar.... He designed us to be tremendously productive and "to mount up with wings like eagles," realistically dreaming of what He can do with our potential.

CAROL KENT

The human heart, has hidden treasures,
In secret kept, in silence sealed;—
The thoughts, the hopes, the dreams, the pleasures,
Whose charms were broken if revealed.

CHARLOTTE BRONTË

I will give you the wealth that is stored away and the hidden riches so you will know I am the Lord, the God of Israel, who calls you by name.

ISAIAH 45:3 NCV

Natural Wonders

If we are cheerful and contented, all nature smiles...the flowers are more fragrant, the birds sing more sweetly, and the sun, moon, and stars all appear more beautiful and seem to rejoice with us.

ORISON SWETT MARDEN

What a wildly wonderful world, God! You made it all, with Wisdom at your side, made earth overflow with your wonderful creations.... All the creatures look expectantly to you to give them their meals on time. You come, and they gather around; you open your hand and they eat from it.... Take back your Spirit and they die, revert to original mud; Send out your Spirit and they spring to life.

PSALM 104:24-30 THE MESSAGE

Beauty puts a face on God. When we gaze at nature, at a loved one, at a work of art, our soul immediately recognizes and is drawn to the face of God.

MARGARET BROWNLEY

The Gift of Family

One of the greatest gifts
That life can give to anyone
Is the very special love that families share...
As years go by,
It's good to know that there will always be
Certain people in our lives who care.
For there are countless things
That only families have in common
And memories that no one else can make...
And these precious ties that bind a family together
Are bonds that time and distance cannot break.

CRAIG S. TUNKS

When you look at your life, the greatest happinesses
are family happinesses.

JOYCE BROTHERS

Promises for Me

Let love and faithfulness never leave you;
bind them around your neck,
write them on the tablet of your heart.

PROVERBS 3:3 NIV

Simple Things

Blue skies with white clouds on summer days. A myriad of stars on clear moonlit nights. Tulips and roses and violets and dandelions and daisies. Bluebirds and laughter and sunshine and Easter. See how He loves us!

ALICE CHAPIN

It's simple things, like a glowing sunset, the sound of a running stream or the fresh smell in a meadow that cause us to pause and marvel at the wonder of life, to contemplate its meaning and significance. Who can hold an autumn leaf in their hand, or sift the warm white sand on the beach, and not wonder at the Creator of it all?

WENDY MOORE

God hasn't invited us into a disorderly, unkempt life but into something holy and beautiful—as beautiful on the inside as the outside.

1 THESSALONIANS 4:7 THE MESSAGE

Hope for Today

Hope begins in the dark, the stubborn hope that if you just show up and try to do the right thing, the dawn will come. You wait and watch and work: You don't give up.

ANNE LAMOTT

This I call to mind and therefore I have hope: Because of the Lord's great love we are not consumed, for his compassions never fail. They are new every morning; great is your faithfulness.

LAMENTATIONS 3:21-23 NCV

Do not spoil what you have by desiring what you have not; but remember that what you now have was once among the things you only hoped for.

EPICURUS

It is difficult to say what is impossible, for the dream of yesterday is the hope of today and the reality of tomorrow.

ROBERT H. GODDARD

Cultivate Joy

Joy is the feeling of grinning on the inside.

MELBA COLGROVE

How necessary it is to cultivate a spirit of joy. It is a psychological truth that the physical acts of reverence and devotion make one feel devout. The courteous gesture increases one's respect for others. To act lovingly is to begin to feel loving, and certainly to act joyfully brings joy to others which in turn makes one feel joyful. I believe we are called to the duty of delight.

DOROTHY DAY

Serve each other with love. The whole law is made complete in this one command: "Love your neighbor as you love yourself."

GALATIANS 5:13-14 NCV

*Since you get more joy out of giving joy to others,
you should put a good deal of thought into the happiness
that you are able to give.*

ELEANOR ROOSEVELT

Of Great Value

Are not five sparrows sold for two pennies? Yet not one of them is forgotten by God. Indeed, the very hairs of your head are all numbered. Don't be afraid; you are worth more than many sparrows.

LUKE 12:6-7 NIV

For God bought you with a high price. So you must honor God with your body.

1 CORINTHIANS 6:20 NLT

For you know that it was not with perishable things such as silver or gold that you were redeemed...but with the precious blood of Christ.

1 PETER 1:18-19 NIV

You are in the Beloved...therefore infinitely dear to the Father, unspeakably precious to Him.

NORMAN F. DOWTY

The Rhythm of My Spirit

Teach me, Father, how to go
Softly as the grasses grow;
Hush my soul to meet the shock
Of the wild world as a rock....
Let the dry heart fill its cup,
Like a poppy looking up;
Let life lightly wear her crown,
Like a poppy looking down,
When its heart is filled with dew,
And its life begins anew.

EDWIN MARKHAM

The time is coming when the true worshipers will
worship the Father in spirit and truth, and that time is
here already. You see, the Father too is actively seeking
such people to worship him. God is spirit, and those who
worship him must worship in spirit and truth.

JOHN 4:23-24 NCV

God knows the rhythm of my spirit and knows my heart thoughts. He is as close as breathing.

Real Joy

I've grown to realize the joy that comes from little victories is preferable to the fun that comes from ease and the pursuit of pleasure.

LAWANA BLACKWELL

Real joy comes not from ease or riches or from the praise of men, but from doing something worthwhile.

SIR WILFRED GRENFELL

*Joyful are people of integrity,
who follow the instructions of the LORD.
Joyful are those who obey his laws
and search for him with all their hearts.*

PSALM 119:1-2 NLT

There is no greater joy nor greater reward than to make a fundamental difference in someone's life.

MARY ROSE MCGEADY

*May the God of hope fill you with all joy and peace as
you trust in him, so that you may overflow with hope.*

ROMANS 15:13 NIV

Today and Always

Some say "tomorrow" never comes,
A saying oft thought right;
But if tomorrow never came,
No end were of "tonight."
The fact is this, time flies so fast,
That e'er we've time to say
"Tomorrow's come," presto! behold!
"Tomorrow" proves "today."

Even though on the outside it often looks like things are
falling apart on us, on the inside, where God is making
new life, not a day goes by without his unfolding grace.
These hard times are small potatoes compared to the coming
good times, the lavish celebration prepared for us. There's
far more here than meets the eye. The things we see now are
here today, gone tomorrow. But the things we can't see now
will last forever.

2 CORINTHIANS 4:16-18 THE MESSAGE

Light tomorrow with today.
ELIZABETH BARRETT BROWNING

....

....

....

....

....

....

....

....

....

....

....

....

God Listens

Open wide the windows of our spirits and fill us full of light; open wide the door of our hearts, that we may receive and entertain Thee with all our powers of adoration.

CHRISTINA ROSSETTI

We come this morning—
Like empty pitchers to a full fountain,
With no merits of our own,
O Lord—open up a window of heaven...
And listen this morning.

JAMES WELDON JOHNSON

God listens in compassion and love, just like we do when our children come to us. He delights in our presence.

RICHARD J. FOSTER

*I love the LORD because he hears my voice
and my prayer for mercy. Because he bends down to listen,
I will pray as long as I have breath!*

PSALM 116:1-2 NLT

Nature's Treasure

If we are children of God, we have a tremendous treasure in nature and will realize that it is holy and sacred. We will see God reaching out to us in every wind that blows, every sunrise and sunset, every cloud in the sky, every flower that blooms, and every leaf that fades.

OSWALD CHAMBERS

If anyone belongs to Christ, there is a new creation. The old things have gone; everything is made new! All this is from God.

2 CORINTHIANS 5:17-18 NCV

The day is done, the sun has set,
Yet light still tints the sky;
My heart stands still
In reverence,
For God is passing by.

RUTH ALLA WAGER

*Something deep in all of us yearns for God's beauty,
and we can find it no matter where we are.*

SUE MONK KIDD

....

....

....

....

....

....

....

....

....

....

....

The Attention of God

We have been in God's thought from all eternity, and in His creative love, His attention never leaves us.

MICHAEL QUOIST

Because God is responsible for our welfare, we are told to cast all our care upon Him, for He cares for us. God says, "I'll take the burden—don't give it a thought—leave it to Me." God is keenly aware that we are dependent upon Him for life's necessities.

BILLY GRAHAM

You are God's created beauty and the focus of His affection and delight.

JANET L. WEAVER SMITH

Give all your worries to him; because he cares about you.
1 PETER 5:7 NCV

The Grand Essentials

The grand essentials of happiness are: something to do, something to love, and something to hope for.

ALLAN K. CHALMERS

Prayer is essential.... Pray hard and long. Pray for your brothers and sisters. Keep your eyes open. Keep each other's spirits up so that no one falls behind.

EPHESIANS 6:18 THE MESSAGE

This is the true joy of life, the being used up for a purpose recognized by yourself as a mighty one; being a force of nature instead of a feverish, selfish little clot of ailments and grievances, complaining that the world will not devote itself to making you happy. I am of the opinion that my life belongs to the community, and as long as I live, it is my privilege to do for it what I can.

GEORGE BERNARD SHAW.

It is only with the heart that one can see rightly.
What is essential is invisible to the eye.

ANTOINE DE SAINT-EXUPÉRY

Unique Gifts

God has a wonderful plan for each person He has chosen. He knew even before He created this world what beauty He would bring forth from our lives.

LOUIS B. WYLY

Everyone has a unique role to fill in the world and is important in some respect. Everyone, including and perhaps especially you, is indispensable.

NATHANIEL HAWTHORNE

Live out your God-created identity. Live generously and graciously toward others, the way God lives toward you.

MATTHEW 5:48 THE MESSAGE

God gives us all gifts, special abilities that we are entrusted with developing to help serve Him and serve others.

God has given gifts to each of you from his great variety of spiritual gifts...so that God's generosity can flow through you.

1 PETER 4:10 NLT

....

....

....

....

....

....

....

....

....

....

....

Promises for Me

Promise Journal

© 2010 Ellie Claire Gift & Paper Corp.

www.ellieclaire.com

978-1-935416-52-4

Compiled by Barbara Farmer & Joanie Garborg

Designed by Mick Thurber

Printed in China